Pure and Chased

Pure and Chased

by
Lyman Hinckley Rose

CFI
Springville, Utah

ISBN: 1-55517-774-3
e. 1

Published by CFI
An Imprint of Cedar Fort Inc.
www.cedarfort.com

Distributed by:

Typeset by Natalie Roach
Cover design by Nicole Shaffer
Cover design © 2004 by Lyle Mortimer

Printed in the United States of America
10 9 8 7 6 5 4 3 2 1
Printed on acid-free paper

Library of Congress Cataloging-in-Publication Data

Rose, Lyman Hinckley, 1958-
    Pure and chased / by Lyman Hinckley Rose.
        p. cm.
    ISBN 1-55517-774-3 (alk. paper)
    1. Chastity--Juvenile literature. 2. Sexual abstinence--Religious
aspects--Christianity--Juvenile literature. 3. Sexual ethics for teenagers. 4.
Dating--Religious aspects--Christianity--Juvenile literature. 5. Sex--Religious
aspects--Christianity--Juvenile literature. 6. Christian teenagers--Sexual
behavior--Juvenile literature. I. Title.

    BV4647.C5R575 2004
    241'.66--dc22
                                    2004020355

Dedication

To the youth of ZION who are called upon in these troubling times to keep the faith, remain pure and prepare the world for the coming of the Lord. May they see the power in purity.

Acknowledgments

I would like to acknowledge my wife Lesa for the wonderful example of purity she is to our nine children. She is a teacher without equal who has helped me with this work, but more importantly, has set our children's feet on the path to purity.

Table of Contents

Introduction
Why the Need for This Book?

It is important to know that there are certain standards that never change. No matter how long the world turns, an inch will always be an inch! A right angle will always be ninety degrees. A pound will always be a pound. The standards of the Lord are even more unchanging. Adultery will never be OK and it will never fall within His laws to commit murder.

It is also important to know that YOU ARE A CHILD OF GOD! I hope you really understand what that means! Most people on the earth find themselves in difficult circumstances with the law of chastity because they have a low self image. They feel that they are not good enough to be accepted by others. As a result, when someone shows an interest in them, they are willing to do almost anything in order to keep that interest intact.

I recently talked with a woman who works in a high school that is attended only by girls who have children and are high school age or younger. There are currently three girls in the school that are thirteen years old and have their own children! There are many others in very difficult circumstances who are trying to be kids but have babies of their own. It is never an easy task. She told me that in virtually every case, the initial problem was a low self-esteem.

How I wish that every young girl or boy could catch the vision that GOD IS THEIR FATHER! How could you have a low self-esteem knowing that you are a literal child of God and as such, you have the potential to become like Him? Not only are you one of His children, but you are one of His chosen children! He has reserved His most choice spirits to come to the earth at this time. You have been held on high awaiting your appointed time to appear on the earth and complete all that He has asked you to do. Of all of the numberless worlds created by Him, His most elect children will come to this earth and they will come during the last days. We are in the last days and YOU are His elect!

Don't let the world convince you that you are anything less. Don't let the adversary persuade you that you have no value and you will never amount to much. We may not amount to much in the eyes of the world. We may not have houses and cars and servants to surround us, but we will become like God if we desire it and work at it.

This is the long way of saying that I hope you will not fall into carnal sins in order to become accepted by those who would prey on your feelings of personal doubt. Instead strive to be received by Him whose child you are in the Highest of His glories.

1

Chastity?

"But ye are a chosen generation, a royal priesthood, an holy nation, a peculiar people; that ye should shew forth the praises of him who hath called you out of darkness into his marvellous light" (1 Pet. 2:9).

Why are we considered peculiar? What makes us different from others?

Isn't it amazing that in the world there are more than 3,000 adolescent pregnancies daily? It's hard to believe. That adds up to more than one million each year! Statistically, 75% of high school students have had some kind of sexual encounter with the opposite sex. That number jumps to almost 85% for college students! More than 4,000 young people lose their virtue every day. That's about one every twenty-one seconds! Currently, about one out of every four births is to an unwed mother! I certainly hope that, at least in this regard, we are indeed a peculiar people.

What is the law of chastity and why should we bother keeping it when it seems to be of so little value to the rest of the world?

The law of chastity is really quite simple. According to

the leaders of the Church of Jesus Christ of Latter-day Saints:

> The power to create children is very sacred. Our Father in Heaven has commanded that the sacred power and privilege of sexual relations be exercised only between a man and woman who are legally married. This is the law of chastity. It means that we must not have sexual relations before we are married, and after we are married we should have sexual relations only with our husband or wife.

It's that simple.

Note that it says "sexual relations," not sexual intercourse. Sexual relations covers a much wider spectrum and is not limited simply to intercourse. Any relations that cause sexual arousal should be kept within the confines of marriage. If it is arousing to kiss, then you should only be kissing your spouse. If holding hands arouses you, then you should only hold hands with your spouse! There is absolutely no safety in playing with these things! If you are dating and spend time hugging and/or kissing to the point of personal arousal, you need to stop immediately and turn off that switch.

Many wonder just how far they can bend the law of chastity without breaking it. The mere asking of the question suggests a desire to push the law to the limits. It's almost like asking just how far you can fall off of a 1,000-foot building before it will cause you trouble. The answer is of course that the first 999 feet won't hurt you but that last one is really a doozy! It's the little things that usually lead up to the big problems.

Falling that last foot off of the building would not be a problem if you started one foot off the ground but when you have 999 feet of speed going in your favor, you've got a problem that you probably cannot escape. Don't do the little things that lead you down the path of sexual relations because once that train has gained a full head of steam and is racing down the track, it is very hard to stop it. It doesn't take much to get the train started and it is extremely powerful once it's started. Once you allow yourself to get started down the track, you find that you pick up speed and force until trying to stop is nearly impossible. Thus it is clear that bending the law of chastity breaks it. When you don't know how far you can go before there is no turning back, it is imperative not to test the law by bending it.

Look at the graph below. It shows a line of progression from holding hands to sexual intercourse. If there are any terms you don't understand here, please take the time today to ask your parents what they mean. If they want to explain it to you, then listen carefully. If they don't think it is the right time, then don't push it and simply realize that each item on the line represents a progression in a relationship.

Holding Hands	Kissing	Heavy Kissing	Light Petting	Heavy Petting	Sexual Intercourse

On the next page I will draw a line from the start to the finish and you need to tell me when to stop. Tell me to stop at a place that you think is OK as far as what you can do without losing control. I know you can't really tell me, but play along so I can continue with the point I am trying to make. The dotted line you will see is my line.

My line

--➤

| Holding Hands | Kissing | Heavy Kissing | Light Petting | Heavy Petting | Sexual Intercourse |

I hope that you noticed instantly that the line was all the way across the graph. I hope you said something to yourself like: "That's way too fast" or, "You didn't give me a chance to stop." The truth is that it *is* very fast and sometimes you might feel like you can't stop. That is the very reason why you must stop immediately if you reach a point where you are becoming aroused. If both of you become aroused at the same time, the line can be drawn so fast that you don't realize that it has gone too far until you are already there.

In my class I have two magnets that are very strong. I have them each on the end of a stick that is about a foot in length. The strength of the magnets represents our sexual desires, which are also very strong. I have a girl and a boy come up to the front of the room and give each of them one of the magnets. I then ask them to get the magnets as close as they can without letting them go all the way together. They try to move them cautiously closer and closer but whenever they get within about an inch or so, they slam together. This is what happens to us if we are both attracted to each other and the power of arousal is strong. It is almost impossible to push the limits and keep from going too far.

Normally, one of the students will eventually turn his or her magnet over so the magnetic field is reversed and the magnets repel each other. They say, "Look, we can't even get close now." They think that they have ruined my demonstration, but they have actually done exactly what I would have hoped they would do. They have figured out that if one of the people in the relationship knows when to turn around and leave, the power of attraction is put on hold and they can resist the temptation!

You have simply got to be able to turn away if there is any arousal going on. Some may say that it is not possible to turn away from something so tempting. Remember the incredible story of Joseph, the son of Jacob (see Gen. 39). His brothers sold him to some Ishmaelites on their way to Egypt. The Ishmaelites sold him to a man named Potiphar who was an officer to the Pharaoh. Joseph became a ruler in Potiphar's house and was given virtually everything that Potiphar had. Potiphar's wife had an eye for Joseph and continually asked him to "lie with her." She was asking him to have sexual relations with her. Finally, one day, when Joseph entered the house to do some work, she grabbed him and begged him to have sex with her. It must have been very tempting. No one else was in the house. Who would have known? He could have taken full advantage of the situation. Of course, the scriptures tell us that Joseph fled and ran so quickly that Potiphar's wife was left holding his garment in her hand. Talk about a turning magnet!

We must be as resolute as Joseph. We must know when to turn and run if need be. One of my close friends found himself in a dangerous situation while on a date. He parked his truck and left his date in the passenger seat while he went into the fast food restaurant to get some food for both of them. She said she did not want to go in. She said she wanted to redo some of her makeup. When he returned to the truck and opened the door, he found his date had removed all of her clothing! The girl he was out with was a beautiful cheerleader who he had been trying to get a date with for months. What would the other guys at school think if he did nothing? Would he be considered a fool if he did not take advantage of the situation? None of that mattered! All that mattered to him was that he knew exactly what his standards were and he knew what he had to do. He had to be like Joseph and turn away. He closed the door and told her to get dressed. After giving her ample time and finding her dressed when he opened the door again, he took her home and the date was over.

The great difficulty though is usually not in the blatant exposure to potential sin. The real difficulty is when we are encouraged to slip slowly down one almost imperceptible step at a time into the pool of sin. We slowly get our toes in and stay at that level until we are comfortable with the temperature of the water. We carefully take another step, sometimes without even noticing our progress. We get in up to our ankles without noticing a change. The water still seems fine and we are nowhere near drowning—we are just ankle deep! Soon we find ourselves in up to our knees. Perhaps we have seen a little bit of the descent but it has not caused any worry because, after all, our heads are still a mile above water and we would never be stupid enough to go in over our heads! We might be a little shocked to be able to feel the water with our hands, that means that the water is almost waist high. That's OK—I'm still not drowning. I can turn back anytime and quickly walk back up the steps and climb out of the pool. While we are thinking about our ability to easily get out if we wanted to, we find that we have gotten up to our elbows. We seem to be walking down the steps a little bit faster than when we started but it's OK—we can still get out. Then, the almost unthinkable happens. We have to take a step and there is none! All we find is a total drop off and we plunge in without control.

When I was a young man, probably about 13 or 14, my father and I went to visit my uncle. When no one answered the front door, we walked around the side of the house to the pool in the back yard. There was my uncle, enjoying a drink of lemonade in a lounge chair. He got out of the chair and said hello to my dad and stuck his hand out to shake my hand. I took his hand and he gripped my hand like a vice. Suddenly, without any warning, he turned around and, making his arm like a whip, he threw me into the pool, clothes and all. I could not swim so I was terrified. He had thrown me in far enough that I had landed on the slope between the shallow and deep ends of the pool. I reached my feet down and I could barely touch the bottom. With the force of his throw, I was still moving toward the deep end and I could feel my feet slowly losing grip on the bottom. Sheer panic overcame me and I was almost certain that I was going to drown. My clothes felt very heavy and seemed to be dragging me further toward the deep end. I began to wave my arms frantically, trying to avoid slipping any further toward the deep end. After what seemed like an eternity, I finally stopped my momentum toward the deep end and began to make ever so slow progress toward the shallow end. This was only after I had literally sunk to the point that my nose and eyes were the only things out of the water! Although it seemed like forever to me, it all happened so fast that my dad did not even have time to take off his shoes as he was going to jump in and get me. He knew I could not swim. When I finally got control and was moving in the right direction, I got my mouth out of the water and told dad not to worry, that I would be able to get out. We never did go visit that uncle again! My point is that I cannot find adequate words to describe the panic I felt when I began slipping into the deep end of that pool. Neither can I describe appropriately the incredible relief I felt when I finally got turned around and was heading in the right direction.

I found out rather unexpectedly that you can't get into the pool without getting wet. It doesn't really matter if you slowly get in or if you go off the diving board—you can't get into the pool without getting wet! The only safe way to avoid getting wet is to stay out of the pool. Stay away from the fence that secures the pool. Don't even think about the pool. OK, you get my point. Turn away if you are the least bit aroused—don't go on or you might drown! Ben Franklin said, "It's easier to suppress the first desire than to satisfy all that follow" (*The Way to Wealth* by Benjamin Franklin, July 7, 1757).

Similarly, Solomon said in the Proverbs:

Can a man take fire in his bosom, and his clothes not be burned? Can one go upon hot coals, and his feet not be burned? So he that goeth in to his neighbour's wife; whosoever toucheth her shall not be innocent. Men do not despise a thief, if he steal to satisfy his soul when he is hungry; But if he be found, he shall restore sevenfold; he shall give all the substance of his house. But whoso committeth adultery with a woman lacketh understanding: he

that doeth it destroyeth his own soul. A wound and dis-
honour shall he get; and his reproach shall not be wiped
away (Proverbs 6:27-33).

In the document entitled *The Family: A Proclamation to the
World*, the First Presidency and the council of the Twelve
Apostles said this:

> The first commandment that God gave to Adam and Eve
> pertained to their potential for parenthood as husband
> and wife. We declare that God's commandment for His
> children to multiply and replenish the earth remains in
> force. We further declare that God has commanded that
> the sacred powers of procreation are to be employed only
> between man and woman, lawfully wedded as husband
> and wife. We declare the means by which mortal life is
> created to be divinely appointed. We affirm the sanctity of
> life and of its importance in God's eternal plan. . . . The
> family is ordained of God. Marriage between man and
> woman is essential to His eternal plan. Children are enti-
> tled to birth within the bonds of matrimony, and to be
> reared by a father and a mother who honor marital vows
> with complete fidelity. . . . We warn that individuals who
> violate covenants of chastity, who abuse spouse or off-
> spring, or who fail to fulfill family responsibilities will one
> day stand accountable before God.

It is not only appropriate, but a commandment that men
and women have sexual relations only within the proper
bonds of marriage. That is what creates families, the basic
unit of the gospel. Without families and the relationships that
create them, the entire plan of salvation would be thwarted.
The desires for intimate relations are strong, natural, and
good. They must be strong in order to entice men and

women to undertake the responsibility of a family. They must be bridled as far as their outward expression until you have been properly married by proper authority and, I would hope, in the proper place, even the House of the Lord, sealed for time and all eternity.

There are many who say that it isn't anyone else's business if they decide to break the law of chastity because, after all, they are only hurting themselves. I don't know of a more selfish attitude than this. They don't think about the potential baby to be born. They think not of the tremendous strain on their parents. They don't consider the feelings of their "partner" and all of the legal issues that can arise and tear families apart. They never even give a thought to the person somewhere in the world who they might have married had they not crossed the line. All they are interested in is the here and now and what will give them pleasure. They don't realize that if they become pregnant or father a child as an adolescent, they will be giving up some of the best and potentially most carefree years of their lives. They don't consider what they will give up if they give in.

Think how you would feel if you kept yourself free from sexual sin and you were waiting to find your future spouse who you hoped had done the same and they hadn't. It is important to realize that when you are out on a date with someone, you are most likely out on a date with someone else's spouse! Unless you marry the person you are out on the date with, you are out on a date with someone else's future spouse. You must be careful and treat those who you date as though you were preparing them for their own future spouse. How would you like the man or woman who is dating your future spouse to treat them? Hopefully, you would want them to be treated with respect and as the child of God that they really are. We must remember that whoever you are out with is someone's son or daughter. They might be someone's brother or sister. They will probably eventually be someone's mother or father. How would you want someone who is dating your brother or sister or mother or father to act? Of course, most importantly is that whoever you are dating is a child of God the Father and a brother or sister of Jesus Christ. Think how they would want you to treat their relative! Remember that no matter how dark the room or how secluded the corner, God is in the car, room, park, etc. with you every second. He is looking at you and knows everything you are doing. So just stay out of the pool until the time is right.

Now I want you to try a little experiment. Get out a piece of paper and draw a line down the middle of the paper. At the top of one column write the word GOOD. At the top of the other column write the words NOT GOOD. Under the "GOOD" column I want you to list things that would help you to keep the law of chastity. Then I want to to list things in the "NOT GOOD" column that would cause you to break the law of chastity. Go ahead and do this right now. Don't go on until you have done this and have at least five things in each column. Let me give you a few ideas to help. Maybe in the GOOD column you would have things like: a love of God, a testimony of the law of chastity, a virtuous girlfriend or boyfriend, or promptings of the Holy Ghost. In the other column you might have: going too deep into the pool, not having any morals, peer pressure, low self-esteem, or looking for lust instead of love. Now that I have given you so many, I want you to come up with at least three on your own. Do it now. Don't go on until you have assembled both lists.

Now, that you have your list, (and I hope you really did it) simply take your pen or pencil and cross out one letter "o" in each word good. You should now have two columns titled GOD and NOT GOD. Now look at your lists. Does it fit? You will find that God wants us to live the law to its fullest and receive the fullness of joy associated with its proper use. You will also find that Satan wants us to misuse this sacred power and will do everything he can to get us to break that law.

Breaking the law of chastity is just about the most serious thing you can do. It is only outranked by two sins: denying the Holy Ghost and murder. Joseph Smith said this about the denial of the Holy Ghost:

> What must a man do to commit the unpardonable sin? He must receive the Holy Ghost, have the heavens opened unto him, and know God, and then sin against him. After a man has sinned against the Holy Ghost, there is no repentance for him. He has got to say that the sun does not shine while he sees it; he has got to deny Jesus Christ when the heavens have been opened unto him, and to deny the plan of salvation with his eyes open to the truth of it; and from that time he begins to be an enemy (*Documentary History of the Church*, volume 6, pages 302-17).

Murder, of course, is the taking of life itself. Alma, speaking to his son Corianton, said this about the law of chastity, denying the Holy Ghost, and murder.

> And this is not all, my son. Thou didst do that which was grievous unto me; for thou didst forsake the ministry, and did go over into the land of Siron among the borders of the

Lamanites, after the harlot Isabel. Yea, she did steal away the hearts of many; but this was no excuse for thee, my son. Thou shouldst have tended to the ministry wherewith thou wast entrusted. Know ye not, my son, that these things are an abomination in the sight of the Lord; yea, most abominable above all sins save it be the shedding of innocent blood or denying the Holy Ghost? For behold, if ye deny the Holy Ghost when it once has had place in you, and ye know that ye deny it, behold, this is a sin which is unpardonable; yea, and whosoever murdereth against the light and knowledge of God, it is not easy for him to obtain forgiveness; yea, I say unto you, my son, that it is not easy for him to obtain a forgiveness. And now, my son, I would to God that ye had not been guilty of so great a crime. I would not dwell upon your crimes, to harrow up your soul, if it were not for your good. But behold, ye cannot hide your crimes from God; and except ye repent they will stand as a testimony against you at the last day. Now my son, I would that ye should repent and forsake your sins, and go no more after the lusts of your eyes, but cross yourself in all these things; for except ye do this ye can in nowise inherit the kingdom of God. Oh, remember, and take it upon you, and cross yourself in these things (Alma 39:3-9).

God gave us life and it is His to take. When we commit murder, we take a life that we really have no right to take. That is one reason that it is such a serious sin. Why is the law of chastity right up next to that one? It is also God's privilege and sacred power to give life. He has shared it with us but only within the bounds He has set which is within the sanctity of marriage. It is also interesting that when we commit sexual sins it can result in the destruction of the soul. As President Benson put it, "Purity is life giving—unchastity is deadly" (*God Country & Family* p. 5). It sounds like another kind of murder, doesn't it? No wonder this sin is next to murder. Isn't it interesting that we punish people for committing murder and yet, as a society, we seem to embrace committing sexual sins. We have been blinded by the cunning of Satan to such a degree that premarital and extramarital sex is now seen as not only acceptable but almost assumed.

Marion G. Romney briefly related how important the law of chastity was to his father.

I remember how my father impressed the seriousness of unchastity upon my mind. He and I were standing in the railroad station at Rexburg, Idaho, in the early morning of 12 November 1920. We heard the train whistle. In three minutes I would be on my way to Australia to fill a mission. In that short interval my father said to me, among other things, "My son, you are going a long way from home. Your mother and I, and your brothers and sisters, will be with you constantly in our thoughts and prayers; we shall rejoice with you in your successes, and we shall sorrow with you in your disappointments. When you are released and return, we shall be glad to greet you and welcome you back into the family circle. But remember this, my son: we would rather come to this station and take your body off the train in a casket than to have you come home unclean, having lost your virtue" (Marion G. Romney. *Ensign* Sept .1981 pg. 3).

There are those who simply do not understand how grievous a sin sexual sin is. I knew a salesman in a company I worked for who had moved here from out of state. He pulled me aside one day and said he was confused by the actions of a Mormon girl he had been dating. He said that she was willing to have sexual relations with him, even intercourse, but would not drink a cup of coffee with him in the morning. He said that she said something about a 'word of wisdom' and not drinking or smoking and how important that was! I hope you are as shocked by that incident as I was. Sexual gratification has become completely expected and chastity is considered highly unusual by the world.

Many years ago I was told of a stake president who had a young man in his office for a priesthood advancement interview. When the president asked the young man if he was morally clean, the response was yes. The stake president moved on with the interview but felt compelled to come back to the issue of morality. Once again he asked the young man if he was sure that he was morally clean to which the youth responded affirmatively. Again the stake president moved on with the interview and again he felt constrained to return to the topic of morality. Finally he asked the young man what it meant to be morally clean, to which the young man responded, "Well, I haven't caught any diseases yet." I hope that you have a full understanding of what it means to be morally clean! If you have any question, finishing reading this book and talk to your parents and priesthood leaders.

I once had a friend tell me that after he had made a bad moral mistake, he went home and showered for a long time until the water ran cold and he scrubbed and scrubbed but still felt dirty. He could not get rid of the feeling of being filthy. You don't have to try committing moral sin to know that it is bad. Dallin Oaks said, "Come to the barn and eat a bit of fresh manure. You need not experience it to know that it is bad."

The punishment for breaking the law of chastity is severe. Paul said to the Galatians:

> This I say then, Walk in the Spirit, and ye shall not fulfill the lust of the flesh. For the flesh lusteth against the Spirit, and the Spirit against the flesh: and these are contrary the one to the other: so that ye cannot do the things that ye would. But if ye be led of the Spirit, ye are not under the law. Now the works of the flesh are manifest, which are these; Adultery, fornication, uncleanness, lasciviousness, Idolatry, witchcraft, hatred, variance, emulations, wrath, strife, seditions, heresies, Envyings, murders, drunkenness, revellings, and such like: of the which I tell you before, as I have also told you in time past, that they which do such things shall not inherit the kingdom of God (Gal. 5:16-21).

The kingdom of God is at stake!!

Of course there are wonderful blessings for keeping the law. Boyd K. Packer said, "Much of the happiness that may come to you in this life will depend on how you use this sacred power of creation" (*Teach Ye Diligently*, p. 259).

In the *For The Strength of Youth* pamphlet it says:

> When you obey God's commandment to be sexually pure, you prepare yourself to make and keep sacred covenants in the temple. You prepare yourself to build a strong marriage and to bring children into the world as part of a loving family. You protect yourself from the emotional damage that always comes from sharing physical intimacies with someone outside of marriage (p. 26).

In Section 121 of the Doctrine and Covenenats we read:

> Let thy <u>bowels</u> also be full of charity towards all men, and to the household of faith, and let <u>virtue</u> garnish thy

thoughts unceasingly; then shall thy <u>confidence</u> wax strong in the <u>presence</u> of God; and the doctrine of the priesthood shall distil upon thy soul as the <u>dews</u> from heaven. The Holy Ghost shall be thy constant <u>companion</u>, and thy scepter an unchanging scepter of <u>righteousness</u> and truth; and thy <u>dominion</u> shall be an everlasting dominion, and without compulsory means it shall flow unto thee forever and ever (D&C 121:45-46).

What marvelous blessings—the presence of God, an everlasting dominion, and the constant companionship of the Holy Ghost!

Now for your assignment. The 13th Article of Faith states that we believe in chastity and virtue and that we seek things that are virtuous.

We believe in being honest, true, chaste, benevolent, virtuous, and in doing good to all men; indeed, we may say that we follow the admonition of Paul—We believe all things, we hope all things, we have endured many things, and hope to be able to endure all things. If there is anything virtuous, lovely, or of good report or praiseworthy, we seek after these things (Articles of Faith 13).

Your assignment is to really seek those things that are virtuous. Do not put yourself in a compromising situation. If you find yourself doing anything that is arousing, STOP IT! AND STOP IT RIGHT NOW! This assignment will be ongoing until you are legally and lawfully married— hopefully in the House of the Lord.

2

What is So Magical About Age 16?

So you're 16—now what? In most cases you are old enough to drive, and that is an awesome responsibility. You might feel old enough to start dating, and that can be an even more awesome responsibility. If you go wrong while driving, you can take the physical life of another person. If you go wrong dating, you can alter the spiritual life and eternal destiny of a brother or sister!

In Chapter One we discussed the Law of Chastity and how important it is to keep it. In this chapter we will discuss why we wait until *at least* the age of 16 to do any dating.

There are two basic reasons for dating. The first is to interact socially with the opposite sex. You can learn to have appropriate fun in mixed company. Dating will teach you how to be friendly and have good manners. You will find out just how different boys and girls really are. The second reason for dating is to find an eternal companion to walk and work with side by side throughout all eternity.

Have you been waiting patiently for your 16th birthday so you can go on a date with that guy or girl that has been bugging you or that you can't get off of your mind? I hate to potentially burst your bubble but guess what?—you really aren't any different on your 16th birthday than you were when you were just 15 years and 364 days old! When you go to sleep on the eve of your 16th birthday, you don't go through an abrupt change that suddenly turns you into an age appropriate for dating young men or young women. All you really are is one day older! So what's the big deal if you go out on a date when you are just a day or two away from your 16th birthday?

Once again there are two reasons for the wait. First, the Prophet of the Lord has told you to wait until you are sixteen. In the *For the Strength of Youth* pamphlet we read: "Do not date until you are at least 16 years old. Dating before then can lead to immorality, limit the number of other young people you meet, and deprive you of experiences that will help you choose an eternal partner." That should be enough all by itself! The other reason to wait is that you are simply not ready. Talk to your parents and ask them if they feel like you are ready to start dating. Of course, at your age you know about 1,000 times more than your parents do, but ask them anyway and get their opinion. Then, although it will be hard, take into consideration what they say. They probably know you better than you think. If they feel that you are not ready, that's OK. Again we read from *For the Strength of Youth*: "Not all teenagers need to date or even want to. Many young people do not date during their teen years because they are not yet interested, do not have opportunities, or simply want to delay forming serious relationships. However, good friendships can and should be developed at every age."

Now I have to tell you that if my daughter came to me and began begging me to go on a date with a certain young man before she was sixteen, I would simply say no. If she continued to tell me how much she was waiting for her birthday so she could go out with this certain boy, I would probably tell her that she would be able to go out on a date when she turned forty! Remember that your parents have the final say until you are legally on your own. That means that until you are 18 and living out of the house, paying your own bills, and supporting yourself in every aspect, your parents are the kings and queens of the house and their word is the last word. There really is no room for argument. It is certainly OK to tell them how you feel and what you would like to do, but when they issue a ruling in the house court, it is done and you just need to live with it! Many years from now you will understand that your parents really did not enjoy arguing or fighting with you. They probably had better things to do than to have lengthy discussions with you on what you thought was fair. You will finally understand that the only reason they handled things the way they did was because they loved you more than you could imagine and simply wanted the very best for you! It is a gratifying moment in a parent's life when one of their children finally catches that vision and grasps the understanding of the love of a parent for a child. Sadly, it normally takes the birth of the individual's own child to begin to comprehend that principle.

So for now, you must simply take it on faith that your parents actually have your best interest at heart. It may seem like they are getting some kind of sadistic joy out of humiliating you in front of your peers, but years from now your eyes will be opened and you will see!

The bottom line is, you must wait until you are either

sixteen years old, or are ready to date, whichever comes last!

> Dating and especially steady dating in the early teens is most hazardous. It distorts the whole picture of life. It deprives the youth of worthwhile and rich experiences; it limits friendships; it reduces the acquaintance which can be so valuable in selecting a partner for time and eternity (Spencer W. Kimball, "President Kimball Speaks Out on Morality," *Ensign*, Nov. 1980, 96).

Now, be certain that when you begin dating (whether at age 16 like most or at age 40 like I've told my daughters) you date in groups and you don't pair off. When you are young, there is nothing good that can come from focusing on one person for your dating experience. It will limit your exposure to others and make it difficult to really see what things you like and what you don't. Early dating with one exclusive person can lead to breaking the law of chastity much more easily than group dating.

When you are at the point in your life when it would be appropriate to look for an eternal companion, then you can begin to look at those you date more closely, one at a time. Until then, just don't do it.

Only date in groups that are doing things that are not offensive to the Spirit of the Lord. If you are invited to go watch videos at a friend's house with a bunch of girls and boys, make sure that the movies that will be shown will be appropriate (Winnie the Pooh comes to mind). When you are single dating make sure that you only go with those who inspire you to be a better person and live the commandments. Anyone who tries to debase you or treat you with any amount of disrespect should never be allowed to date you. Always date those who have the same spiritual desires that you have. "Be ye not unequally yoked together with unbelievers: for what fellowship hath righteousness with unrighteousness? and what communion hath light with darkness?" (2 Cor. 6:14).

My mother quickly became very careful about who she would accept a date with because of what her father would do to them. Her father was an Apostle, which would make it hard enough to take her out, but when a date showed up at the house, he would not let his daughter come downstairs until he had given her date a thorough interview! There were a couple of times that Mom came down the stairs and her date for the evening was not there. Her father simply said something like, "He wasn't worthy to take you out." It's no wonder that she became so careful about accepting dates! Now you must be careful, too. Just imagine that your parents are going to interview your dates and let that scare you into making good choices. (Parents, if you are reading this, go ahead and interview your children's dates—it really does wonders for the caliber of dates they have.)

Now a note to you boys—LEARN HOW TO TREAT A LADY!

Now a note to you girls—LEARN HOW TO BE A LADY!

I fully expect my sons to open the door for their dates. I fully expect my daughters to wait by the door until their dates open it for them. Now I know that that sounds like something out of a medieval text book but it shows the respect that a man should have for a woman. These tender creatures are certainly daughters of God. Respecting them as such will clearly direct the way you treat them while on a date. I hope you young men would never pull up to a date's house and honk the horn! If you did that at my house, you would instantly fail the interview!

Now you young girls, you must train these young men early so there is no question about what you expect. I am sure you have heard it said that the man is the head of the household and that is true, but with careful preparation, the woman is the neck and she can turn the head anyway she wants to! I am disturbed by the way girls treat young men today. They almost literally throw themselves at the young men. They offer to drive, to pay for meals and movies, they call constantly and make it well known that they are available. Girls, it is very hard to teach a young man how to be a proper young man when you make it so he doesn't have to! He should be the one pursuing you. He should be trying to convince you that he is the greatest thing since sliced bread. He should be opening doors, paying for dates, and calling you to ask you out. He will never learn how to treat you properly if you don't force him to. If you make it so it takes no effort on his part to win you, then you're lost.

Young men, date the girls that bring out the gentleman in you. Don't fall for the girls who toss themselves in front of you and require no effort on your part. Enjoy the "game" of pursuing your eternal companion. By nature, men are meant to be the hunters, not the hunted. Ask girls out instead of waiting for them to take action. It is a hard thing to do when so many young women are willing to make it so easy, but those girls who respect themselves enough to wait for you to fight for them are well worth the effort!

When you begin dating, go in groups or on double dates. Avoid going on frequent dates with the same person. Make sure your parents meet those you date. You may want to invite your dates to activities with your family. Plan dating activities that are positive and inexpensive and that will help you get to know each other. Do things that will help you and your companions maintain your self-respect and remain close to the Spirit of the Lord.

Here are some dating do's for fun while dating in groups or, when appropriate, as couples:

*Make the decisions to do the right things before you ever make a plan for your first date. You don't need to decide on every date that you will not do inappropriate things. Make that decision now and never break it.

*Relax and have fun. Once you have made your decisions, you can simply enjoy the experience of dating.

*Remember the phrase "the more the merrier" and believe it. Get a good group together and you will form friendships that will last forever.

*Always have a plan for your date. If you do, it is unlikely that you will fall into doing something wrong or improper.

*Only choose things to do that are well within the standards of the church.

*Go to ward activities and don't give in to those who tell you that such activities are dull or aren't fun.

*Be very modest in your dress for dates. Modesty makes everything more comfortable and keeps thoughts where they should be.

*Say your prayers before going on a date. You will be much less likely to do something bad if you pray before you leave.

*Remember that it doesn't have to cost a lot of money to have fun and do something constructive. Go on a fun scavenger hunt, get ice cream and go on a walk, or throw a frisbee.

*Be yourself and have fun. I remember telling a young lady that I was going to take her to a lush green island for dinner and so we ate on a traffic island in the middle of the road. (Well, at least it did have grass and was quite lush)

Now for your assignment. Do not date until you are at least sixteen and then only if you are ready as expressed by your parents! If you are dating and are not ready to be married, keep your dating experiences to group dating. If you are looking for an eternal companion, look high and never concede to anything less than a child of God deserves. If you do these things, you will have a great chance of finding someone who's hand you can hold for time and all eternity.

3

Be Afraid, Be Very Afraid!

Think about the most frightening thing you can imagine—something that makes you so afraid that you almost pass out. My wife used to have a recurring dream about being chased by someone who had a knife and was trying to stab her. What scares you more than anything? How about a six-foot black widow spider chasing you? What about an alien taking you to its ship to do experiments? What about a six-foot alien spider taking you to its web ship for dinner? All right, you get the point—think of something terrifying. Now, multiply that fear and terror by one thousand times and you will have almost reached the level of fear that you should have about pornography.

Pornography can be found in almost every home in the country. It is highly likely that there is pornography in your home right now! Can you find it? Where could you look in order to find it? Hopefully there is not any blatant pornography laying around your house like bad movies or magazines, but it still could be there. A couple of good places to start looking might be by the television or the radio. Have you seen anything pornographic on television lately? I want you to really think about that question. Have you seen anything pornographic on television lately?

To help answer the question, let's define pornography. Pornography is anything produced to arouse sexual desire. Common synonyms are smut, lewdness, obscenity, vulgarity, dirt, and filth. The word pornography actually comes from the Greek word pornographos which means writing about prostitutes.

Now, I ask the question a third time. Have you seen anything pornographic on television lately? Are there any shows you have seen that elude to sexual things either by words, action, or innuendo? What about commercials on TV? Have you seen any that are provocative?

The sad truth is that pornography is almost everywhere! You can't look through a magazine or watch TV without being exposed to it. The cunning thing is that pornography tends to start with little things and then can build up in some cases to total wickedness. It is very similar to drug abuse. Most drug addicts start with something low on the scale of drugs. They use it for awhile and realize that it just doesn't give them the same kick that it did the first time. They either need a little bit more of what they have been using or they need to move up to something more potent. They try slightly harder drugs until they have the same experience again. They keep moving up until they reach the hardest drugs available and still they find that the bang isn't quite as good as before. Then, they solve that problem by simply using more and more of it. They do this until they either can no longer function, or they are forced to withdraw from the drugs. If they do go through the withdrawals, they find their brains forever damaged. They never can get quite back to the level of intelligence or reason that they enjoyed before they gave up their lives to drugs.

It really is an addiction in every sense of the word. Their bodies become chemically dependent on the effects of the drugs.

Pornography has the same effect. People may start off with putting up with the innuendoes on a television show. Before long, they hardly even notice them anymore. They have become casual about things that were offensive the first time they heard them. They no longer have a reaction to it because it has become so commonplace. Then the adversary moves in with something a little more crass and we are offended, but only slightly. If we had been approached with this second level of pornography in the first place, we would have totally shunned it, but now we have been softened by the first level that we have experienced over a period of time. Soon we find ourselves accepting shows into our house that not only condone sexual relations before marriage, but make it the accepted norm. The progression continues and we become more and more numb to the offensive things that are parading before us on a daily basis. We actually become addicted to the emotional surge that sexual content brings.

We don't even realize it, but, like the drug user, our bodies actually undergo a chemical change that causes us to want more and more of this type of stimuli. When we experience pleasurable things, our body produces a chemical in our brain that makes the event that brought the pleasure stick in our memory. That is why when a person sees a pornographic picture, he or she tends to remember it for a long time. We become as addicted to that need for pleasure from the chemical changes in our bodies as the drug addict does to the chemical changes in their bodies. It can reach a point where it is almost impossible to overcome without the assistance of a professional.

Now I want you to closely scrutinize the television programs you watch during this week. Instead of just laying back in the chair and letting them lull you into a state of semi-consciousness, listen to what is going on and look for inappropriate innuendoes. Is sex ever talked about? If it is, is it treated as something sacred between a man and a woman in the bonds of marriage? Or is it joked about or debased and treated as something accepted as normal outside of marriage? What about the situation in the show you are watching? Are there people of the opposite sex living together? Are there people having sex before marriage? Are there homosexual relationships shown to be normal and acceptable? What about the language? Is there anything you would consider inappropriate? Do they talk about sex in a casual manner? What about the wardrobe? Are the females modestly dressed? There are several reality shows that cover everything from marriage and dating, to eating disgusting things, to trying to survive. There are courtroom shows for divorces and shows where people reveal hidden secrets and they end up fighting on the set. If you watch any of these, give them a close look and see if they are uplifting or pornographic. Of course the final scrutiny is simply asking yourself, if the Lord were in the chair next to you, would you change the channel? What would you change it to or would you simply turn it off? Then, after looking at it from this perspective for an entire week, ask yourself if pornography has found a way into your own house!

Let's tackle potentially the largest contributor to pornography in a home next to television. As a matter of fact, this one could be bigger because it has the ability to bring the blatant horrible kind of pornography right into our homes. Of course I am talking about the Internet!

When I was young, there was a theater in downtown Salt Lake City that showed X-rated movies. It was called the Studio Theater. As a kid, all I remember about it was seeing the marquee that simply said "X-Rated." As I got a little bit older I remember seeing the same sign that now said "XX-Rated." As a teenager, I remember it saying "XXX-Rated." I don't know if the movies just kept getting more graphic or if the owner just wanted the patrons to think they were. At that time, there were virtually no video stores. If you wanted pornographic movies, you simply had to go to the one or two theaters in town that showed them. I had friends in high school that went to a few of these movies and told me how horrible they were. Although I was invited a couple of times to go, the thought of being in the same room with several sexual deviants was more than enough to keep me from accepting the invitation. I had also decided long before that I would never go anyway.

After the era of the X-Rated theater came the invention of the video. This caused a great boom in the pornography industry. Suddenly, you didn't need to go to a sleazy theater to see this filth. Now you just had to embarrass yourself in front of the clerk at the video store instead of in front of several other X-Rated theater patrons. This made it easier to obtain and view pornography. In fact, this is one of the things that caused the early success of video stores which were having some difficulty being accepted for mainstream videos. The profits from the rental and sale of pornographic videos allowed some of the stores to stay in business long enough for the general public to become more accepting of renting normal movies and the industry survived.

The next link in the chains of hell and potentially the most threatening has been the advent of the Internet. Now perversion is at your fingertips! You don't need to be embarrassed by the store clerk or the theater junkies. You can, in the privacy of your own home, bring the most filthy pornography right onto your computer screen. Here are some startling statistics from Dr. Victor Cline who is presently a psychotherapist specializing in family/marital counseling and sexual addictions.

The following statistics reflect Internet pornography use in the United States:
- Nearly 20 million individuals are accessing the top five pay Internet porn sites per month.
- Nearly 100 million individuals are accessing the top five free porn sites per month.
- Nearly 17 percent of Internet users have problems with sexual addictions.
- About 70 percent of those accessing porn sites on the Internet do it weekdays between 9 a.m. and 5 p.m.— during working hours.
- There are now more than 100,000 Web sites dedicated to selling sex on the Internet—which does not include chat rooms, e-mail or other forms of sexual contact on the Web.
- There are about 200 sex-related Web sites added each day

to the Internet.
- Sex on the Internet constitutes the third largest economic sector on the Web, generating more than a billion dollars annually.

(Source: Victor B. Cline, Nov. 29, 2003. LDS *Church News* p. Z04.)

Never before in the history of the world has it been so easy to bring the most despicable, vile pornography into our homes. All it takes is an Internet hookup and a few mouse clicks. The thing that makes it much worse than ever before is that now the more than 100,000 Web sites dedicated to pornography on the internet are battling for advertising dollars! That means that they are constantly trying to outdo each other in order to bring in more viewers. They have tried and will continue to try everything and anything that is so shocking or horrible or enticing that they can get the highest click through rate so they can charge their advertisers more and more to be on their site. This means that the perversions just keep getting grosser and more disgusting all the time. I would dare to suggest that the pornography that is on the internet today is much more lurid than what was showing in the Studio Theater even when it said XXX-Rated!

You simply cannot let the Internet lead you to pornography. There are some simple rules to follow in order to keep this filth off of your computer:
—Place your computer in a high-traffic area of your home like the family room.
—Always face the computer screen to the room and not to the wall.
—Use passwords to get onto the computer that only a

competent adult knows so that children cannot get on the computer without a parent knowing.

—Share the computer with each other—use a buddy system so that no one is ever on it completely alone.

—Make certain that you do not open any e-mail that looks the least bit questionable.

The Internet literally opens the world to our view and can bring us many wonderful, positive things. It can also drag us down to hell and ensnare us in its web if we are not careful. Now think about your Internet use—has this been an avenue for pornography to get into your home? You decide and then take appropriate action.

Music can also have an astounding effect on us. When we hear words put to music, we tend to remember them for a much longer time than if we hear words alone. That is why so many companies have jingles for their products. It makes us remember it for a long time. What is in the music you listen to? What will you remember for a long time?

Recently a young woman told me about an experience she had in college. She went to a religious college and on the weekends she and her roommates would go to a dance club and have a blast dancing to what she referred to as a "great beat." She said it was fun to dance to and she and her friends weren't listening to the words of the songs—they just loved the beat. Her wise father gave her the counsel to listen to the words and to realize that those words were entering her mind no matter how subtle it was. When she focused on the words, she was appalled at what was being said and what she had been letting into her mind subconsciously. She felt a huge burden lift from her when she stopped going to the clubs and her spirit was healed.

You may think that you don't hear the words or that you are not letting them into your mind, but beware. Your mind is highly powerful and can retain messages and words at a subconscious level that you never see or hear on a conscious level. The curious thing is that when a message is in the subconscious, it is more powerful at causing action than when it is noted consciously. In 1952 a movie came out called *Picnic* and it was shown in many theaters throughout the country. During the movie a picture of a particular cola drink would flash on the screen for much less than a second. It was so fast that the conscious mind didn't even see it and had no recollection of it, but drink sales went through the roof because the subconscious saw and remembered it and desired it. This is called subliminal advertising and it is illegal to use to sell a product because it bypasses your ability to reason and goes right to your subconscious, causing you to take action that seems beyond your control. I have heard of department stores that play their usual low key mellow music over the public address system but they slip in words like "shoplifting doesn't pay" and "if you steal you will go to jail." No one hears the words on a conscious level, but the subconscious picks them up and responds. This type of subliminal messaging is legal and is used because it decreases shoplifting.

Well, music does the same thing with tremendous power. A song can put thoughts into your mind on a subconscious level that can cause action almost beyond your control. Don't you think it is up to you to find out what those messages are? During this week take the time to listen to the words of the music you enjoy. If you can't hear the words or figure out what is being said, look up the words on the Internet or find the CD and see if the words are written on the insert. Find out what is going into your mind and potentially taking control. Now I ask you to determine if any of the words are pornographic in nature. Do they talk inappropriately about sexual relations? Do they express sexual desires? You make the call! Has pornography found another foothold in your personal life?

Now I mentioned dancing above, so let's talk briefly about it. If you have seen any old movies with dancing in them, you can tell that dancing has changed significantly over the past several decades. We have gone from waltzing to wild and from square dancing to slam dancing. Instead of just touching hands, we are touching anything and everything. This is all in the progression towards unrighteous things. In music videos there are so many pornographic things that it would take a book to discuss them all. I have seen clips of some music videos on commercials and with the hip thrusts and other moves I am amazed that the performers are not all in traction! Many music videos are almost pure pornography. We simply cannot allow them into our homes.

When I was young and we would have a church dance, we were told to make sure that there was daylight between us and the girls we were dancing with, especially during the slow dances. Now it's hard to find a place to go dancing that has any daylight at all! Most dance clubs are dark places and can leave you with a dark feeling. I suggest that when you are dancing you leave enough space between you and your partner to fit a Book of Mormon, and that you make sure that you are dancing in such a way and at such a place that the sight of the Book of Mormon, if it were really there, would not make you uncomfortable! (Remember, I am not talking about the Book of Mormon on CD!)

Think about the last dance that you attended. What kind of experience was it? How did you feel when you left the dance? Was there anything in the music or the dancing that, according to our definition, was pornographic?

Let's talk about modesty for a moment. Do you think that your clothes are pornographic? Remember our definition—anything produced to arouse sexual desire. Does your clothing turn heads for the wrong reason? Is it revealing because it is tight or shows too much skin? We will actually be addressing modesty more completely in the next chapter, but think about what you wear.

Now just a quick note on language. Your vocabulary and the things you talk about tells those around you a lot about you. It reveals some of your intellect and ability but most importantly it can reveal your spirituality. If you tell off-color or dirty jokes, that can be a type of pornography. Don't use humor to make fun of sacred things. Never use the names of deity casually or disrespectfully. Examine your language and if it needs a cleaning, give it a good scrubbing.

Magazines are another source of pornography. I am not talking about "pornographic" magazines. I am talking about the everyday magazines that you might see on the table while waiting for a haircut or at the auto repair shop. There are ads in magazines now that would have had to appear in pornographic magazines just 20 years ago. There are articles in youth magazines that discuss things of a sexual nature and they almost always do it from a standpoint that does not follow Church doctrine. I was shocked and amazed recently when I went to have tires put on my car and as I sat in the waiting room, I picked up the magazine that was in the chair I was going to sit in. I sat down and opened it. It did not look very "bad." It was a magazine for young girls and, having young girls, I thought maybe this would be a fun thing to subscribe to for them. I began to look at the list of articles and quickly put it down in disgust. There was an article on hiding your sexual experiences from your parents. There was another one on the benefits of self-stimulation. This was pornography pure and simple. How that kind of smut can be allowed to pass for mainstream magazine material is unbelievable. I took down the phone number on the inside cover of the magazine and called them when I got home and let them know how repulsed I was. Their response was very troubling. They simply said that they would not change what they were doing because that is the kind of thing that young girls want and need to know! Be extremely careful what you look at and read in any magazines. Look at every magazine in your house right now and look through it carefully. Do they contain any ads, stories, or articles that are pornographic? If so, get rid of them so the Spirit can return.

The final item on our list of pornography is movies. From my earlier mention of the Studio Theater, it is obvious that there are strong pornographic movies out there. I hope that is not a problem for you and I hope they are not in your home. But what about R-rated movies? Are they pornographic? The living prophet has told us not to watch R-rated movies. Do we need to know more than that? An R rating doesn't stand for "reverent" or "righteous." The "R" stands for "restricted" because of objectionable content. The world feels that we should be restricted from seeing inappropriate things until we are 17. Well, smut is smut no matter how old you are. Pornography doesn't stop being pornography when you hit a certain age—it always was and always will be filth and smut and improper!

What about PG-13 movies? In our house we have a rule that Mom or Dad has to see a PG-13 movie and approve it before any of the kids can see it. If my wife and I don't want to see it because of the title or an ad we have seen for it, there is no discussion—we don't allow it. Now that may sound harsh but we have several years of experience behind us and it has been very rare that we have seen a PG-13 movie that we thought was OK for family viewing. The same rule applies for PG movies. Our measuring stick is simply to ask "if the Lord were watching it with us, would we be comfortable?"

Movies have a way of sneaking things in that we normally would not allow in our homes. I still remember my 80-year-old aunt calling my mother on the phone and telling her about a movie that she had seen that was one of the best movies my aunt had ever seen. My mother asked her why it had the rating it did and my aunt said that there was one part that was bad but the rest was so good that it was worth it. My mom never went and I thank her for that example to me.

In my book *Dare to Prepare*, I discuss going to this kind of movie by referring to a story from an old stake leader. He brought brownies to an activity and mentioned to us that we could have one if we wanted one. Everyone wanted one of course. Then he told us that while he was making them, he had dropped one rabbit dropping in the mix. He said he didn't know exactly where it was but he was certain it was in there somewhere. Then he asked again if we wanted a brownie. Of course, no one did. Why are we willing to accept a movie with one bad part if we wouldn't eat a brownie? The fact is that if it is bad, it is bad. If the adversary wants to try to sneak a little bit of rabbit dropping into our lives by putting it in an otherwise good movie, we simply can't let him.

Think about the last several movies you either saw in the theater or brought home to view. Was there anything in them that meets our definition of pornography? Think carefully, and then take appropriate action.

Pornography really does kill! It kills your spirit and drives the Holy Ghost away from you. It blocks revelation and can hinder your ability to pray. It can kill you spiritually! Don't let it happen, don't just look the other way—RUN!

> Pornography in all its forms is especially dangerous and addictive. What may begin as a curious indulgence can become a destructive habit that takes control of your life. It can lead you to sexual transgression and even criminal behavior. Pornography is a poison that weakens your self-control, changes the way you see others, causes you to lose the guidance of the Spirit, and can even affect your ability to have a normal relationship with your future spouse. If you encounter pornography, turn away from it immediately (*For the Strength of Youth*).

Remember that if you read it, listen to it, or watch it—you support it.

Several years ago, I and my brothers took our father on a

trip to his old mission field in Denver, Colorado. One of the things we did while we were there was to visit the Denver Mint where millions of dollars in coins are produced. I remember how impressed I was to see the blank coins come through the system to the dye machine which would stamp an image on them. It intrigues me that until that piece of metal was stamped, it have virtually no value, but once stamped it was worth 25¢. The only difference between the two pieces of metal was the impression. If the coin did not receive the right impression, it was cast out of the system to be recycled. the impression took a lot of pressure to stamp correctly on each coin. I hope that what we have discussed in this chapter has made an impression on you, a very heavy impression on you. I hope that it has been of value to you by making the right impression on your mind.

Now for your assignment. Look at all of the things that we have discussed and hold them up to the scrutiny of our definition of pornography. Don't simply pass by anything—really scrutinize everything. If there is pornography in your house, get rid of it! It doesn't matter if it is in the TV shows, music, magazines, videos, Internet, language, or any other aspect of your life—get rid of it before it gets rid of you!

4

You're Just Being Modest

Immodest clothing includes short shorts and skirts, tight clothing, shirts that do not cover the stomach, and other revealing attire. Young women should wear clothing that covers the shoulder and avoid clothing that is low-cut in the front or the back or revealing in any other manner. Young men should also maintain modesty in their appearance. All should avoid extremes in clothing, appearance, and hairstyle. Always be neat and clean and avoid being sloppy or inappropriately casual in dress, grooming, and manners (*For the Strength of Youth*).

It has been very hard over the last several years to find modest clothing, especially for my daughters. I don't know what the fashion designers were thinking when they decided that pants were to be way low on the top and shirts were to be way high on the bottom. They must have thought that pants and shirts don't get along! Of course, most of the bare midriff syndrome comes from current popular stars who wear very revealing clothes. Girls, you must remember that you might call it fashion but if it is revealing, boys call it arousing. Young girls find out early that if they wear certain kinds of clothing, young boys follow them around like puppies. The girls think it is because they look cute and fashionable, but it is really because clothes that are immodest cause that chemical reaction that we talked about earlier that brings on arousal, even if it's in its most mild form. Make sure that you dress in such a way that if you came home from school to find the stake president in your front room, you wouldn't feel like bolting to your bedroom to change into something more conservative.

But it is not just the girls!

I don't know why so many young men have a chronic allergy to belts! I have literally seen a kind of magic going on around the high schools nearby. I know that it is impossible, according to the laws of physics, to have something defy the law of gravity, but I see it all over. Boys wearing their pants literally below their back sides! I don't know how their pants can stay on their legs without any support. They must have velcro on their boxers!

When I was in high school, we used to carry our dirty gym clothes home by stuffing them into one of our gym socks. Occasionally we would get a little rowdy and start a friendly fight smacking each other with the heavy, stuffed socks. I will never forget how embarrassed my friend was when his sock ripped apart while he was swinging it at me and his underwear went sailing down the hall floor and slid right in front of a group of girls. I think if he could have died right there, he would have. As it was, he did not come back to school for several days because of the humiliation of having these girls see his underwear.

Well, how times have changed! Now it is not only OK but quite common that girls see boys' underwear and they see it while the boys are still wearing it! Is this a mark of manhood or the first signs of insanity? I have threatened my boys with having to wear tight suspenders to hold up their pants if they refuse to wear a belt and keep it tight enough to actually hold their pants on. You too must dress appropriately and take heed to the phrase "keep your pants on!" How would you feel if you were passing the sacrament and your pants fell to the ground!?!

Have you ever been to the temple grounds? Have you seen the lovely flowers and the clean sidewalks? Have you noticed that everything seems to be in its right place and well groomed? The temples are always surrounded with the most pleasing and beautiful things possible, things that invite the Spirit. In 1 Cor. 3:16-17 it says: "Know ye not that ye are the temple of God, and that the Spirit of God dwelleth in you? If any man defile the temple of God, him shall God destroy; for the temple of God is holy, which temple ye are." Knowing that you literally are a temple of God, think about how you surround that temple. Is what you wear pleasing, beautiful, and non-offensive to the Spirit? I am convinced that the Lord has visited each of his temples that are made of mortar and brick. Is your temple clean enough both inside and outside to invite the visit of His spirit?

One third of the hosts of heaven did not and never will receive bodies. We should be so grateful for our bodies that we would treasure them and take care of them in the most careful and wonderful way possible.

I had a friend in college who was very conservative in her attire when she first came down to BYU. It took her more liberal roommates a few months, but they finally got her to "loosen up" and start to wear things that were not so conservative. She soon found that her new wardrobe was causing a lot of traffic at their apartment. More and more guys started stopping by just to chat and hang out. She continued to escalate in her immodesty until she had almost surpassed her roommates. Then a tragic thing happened. She was not used to all of the attention she was beginning to receive and she wasn't quite sure how to handle it. One very smooth-talking guy began to come around when the skirts were getting shorter, the tops were getting skimpier and tighter, and the makeup was getting thicker. He started in with his charming approach and, after a few meetings, finally pushed her into a sexual encounter. She basically felt defenseless because she didn't know how to handle this guy's advances. She had never experienced this kind of attention before. She also felt guilty for egging him on with her new, more revealing styles. Ultimately, she felt there was no way back and the last time I saw her, she was lost and confused.

There are some who feel like they will never go on a date or have anyone like them unless they dress in such a way that they immediately attract the opposite sex. This may seem true on the surface, but it is one of Satan's biggest lies! Dressing immodestly will only bring those people around who respond to that type of clothing at a base level. If you want to be surrounded by people who are only interested in the physical aspects of a relationship, then dress provocatively and you will attract them like flies. They will show up thinking that you are also only interested in the physical things and that you will be an easy mark for some kind of physical activity. They seldom have any thoughts of a lasting relationship or of any kind of commitment. They are users and losers who will use you and lose you as fast as they can.

If, on the other hand, your desire is to attract those who want to experience you as more than just a physical person, dress appropriately and modestly. The most attractive girls I have seen have been modestly dressed, are very neat in their clothing, and moderate with their makeup. These girls attract the kind of young men that are looking for someone much deeper than a simple physical desire. They are looking for someone to ultimately spend their eternal lives with and they want someone who can offer love, not lust. Don't feel like you will never date if you dress conservatively. You will not only date, but you will date the right kind of people, the ones you really do want to date.

I have told my girls, "Don't show anything to someone's eyes that you would feel uncomfortable having touched by their hands!" Keep it covered up! I have also advised them that they should wear clothing that would accommodate garments. There are several advantages to this. The first one is that it is very easy to tell if an item of clothing would not cover garments and that makes the decision process much easier. The arguments are brief because a piece of clothing either does or does not pass the "garment test." Secondly, if they always buy clothing that is "garment-worthy," they will not have to redo their entire wardrobe when they do go through the temple!

In 1 Cor. 6:15 it says: "Know ye not that your bodies are the members of Christ? shall I then take the members of Christ, and make them the members of an harlot? God forbid." If our bodies are considered members of Christ and temples of God, let's clothe them properly out of our great love and respect for the Lord.

Both boys and girls need to remember who gave them their bodies and how they should respect them by covering them suitably. Don't let peer pressure cause you to be immodest. Choose friends that support your standards and that dress modestly. If you don't, you could be heading for disaster. But if you do, you could be looking at lifetime of great friendships that will support you and help you throughout your life.

Now for your assignment. I want you to go through your clothing and see if it will pass the "garment test." Consider changing the items that don't pass the test for items that will. Also, think about the type of people you are attracting. Are these the people you want to spend eternity with? Are these the people that will go with you to the temple when the time is right to be sealed forever? If not, think about why they are hanging around with you. Is your wardrobe part of the problem? If so, refer to the first part of your assignment.

5

Consequences

PLEASE MAKE SURE THAT YOU DON'T READ THIS CHAPTER WITHOUT READING CHAPTER 6 AS WELL!

There are two words that can bring the greatest joy or the most exceptional pain on earth. The two words are I'M PREGNANT. Think for a moment how these words might affect you depending on how and when they are uttered. If you are a husband sitting at the dinner table on your first anniversary, what might your response be? What if you are a father or mother and your daughter says she needs to talk to you in private for a minute? What if your girlfriend stops you after school and you ask her if she is feeling OK and that is her response?

When I first heard these two words, I felt such incredible joy in my heart I thought I would burst. My wife told me she was pregnant and I felt a unity with her that I had not felt anywhere before. We shed many tears of happiness for the blessing of being pregnant. For the next several months, I would daydream about how wonderful it was going to be to be a father. What a blessing it was to have a family who would be born in the covenant and off to a good start. I was elated and looked forward with great anticipation to the event of the birth of my first child. While at the hospital for the delivery, I went down to get a drink at the cafeteria and thought to myself, the next time I get a drink, I will be a father! This event was eternal in its implications. I knew that in a few hours I would be a father and I could never not be a father after that, from eternity to eternity. I would now be a father no matter what else happened in my life. I could change being a husband and my wife could change being a wife, but no matter what, neither of us could change being a parent after that day. What an eternal rush it was to think about that!

On the other side of the coin, I had a good friend who heard those two words in a much different place and at a much different time in his life. We were just out of high school and he had been dating a girl for a very short while. They had slipped into the deep end of the pool on only one occasion but it was enough. She told him on one of their dates that she was pregnant and they both cried for hours. Their tears were not tears of happiness—they were tears of sorrow and fear. They planned a quick wedding and tried their best to deal with the situation. There was always doubt in their hearts as to the reason they got married. Was it because of their love for one another? Did they really want to spend either time or eternity with each other? Their marriage finally ended in a divorce and their child has to deal with all of the difficulties associated with that situation.

There are certainly hazards of breaking the law of chastity. An unplanned or unwanted pregnancy is one of them. If a pregnancy has occurred, REMEMBER ABORTION SHOULD NOT BE AN OPTION unless the specific circumstances specified by the Church exist. Those circumstances include if the pregnancy is the result of rape, incest, or if there is a high threat of the mother losing her life. Even in these cases, the mother can choose to carry the baby to term. There are those who feel that it is up to them to decide no matter the circumstances because it is their body. We must remember that our body is a gift from a loving God and it is His privilege to determine the beginning and the end of life. We must also remember that when conception occurs, there is another body growing within its mother and although it is part of her, it is also its own being. Elder Dallin H. Oaks suggests that if a woman makes the choice to be involved in the acts that can cause pregnancy, then her right to choose in the matter has already taken place. She no longer has the right to terminate the pregnancy because she already exercised her right in the taking of the risk of pregnancy ("Weightier Matters," *Ensign* January 2001).

The next thing to remember if there is a pregnancy is that the Church direction is for the father and the mother of the baby to marry if at all possible, and if that is not an option, the baby should be given up for adoption. If you can establish a family with a father and a mother for the child, that is ideal. If you can't, then you should give the child the chance to grow up in an environment with a father and a mother through adoption. I have seen instances where a pregnant mother has been promised by her parents that they will treat their grandchild as their own and that the mother need not look to adoption for the baby. Later, the grandparents, who were taking care of the child because the single mother was working throughout the day, either became too old, died, or had to move away and left the mother in a very difficult situation. It would have been much better for all involved—especially the child—to go through the Church social services adoption process, giving the child the advantage of a two-parent family.

Another potential danger of breaking the law of chastity is the loss of the blessing of going on a mission. Recently, Elder Ballard spoke in General Conference on the subject of "The Greatest Generation of Missionaries" and he told us that the bar has been raised for missionary service. He said that we cannot freely sin and then think that we will repent when we are 18 1/2 years old and go on our mission. (See *Ensign* Nov. 2002) It is possible that the frequent breaking of the law of chastity will cost you the opportunity of serving a mission. A mission can be the most beneficial two years you could spend on planet earth and the chance to go might vanish because of sin.

I had several friends who were unable to go on missions because of their poor ability to keep the law of chastity. They missed the blessings of serving and sharing the gospel that cannot be recovered. If you want to make sure you are worthy to go, BE WORTHY!!

Of course you will also lose the Spirit of the Lord if you are in sin. His Spirit simply can't dwell in an unholy temple. The lack of the Spirit can dull your senses and cause you to forget who you really are and why you are really here on earth. The Spirit is your guide and friend. After you were baptized, the person who confirmed you a member of the Church probably said words very similar to "receive the Holy Ghost." This is not only a priesthood ordinance giving you access to the Holy Ghost, it is also an admonition for you to accept the Holy Ghost in your life. Literally you are to receive Him. In order to receive the Holy Ghost you must keep your life in order and clean from sin so He can dwell in you and direct your paths. If you reject instead of receive Him by committing sins, you will no longer be able to feel His presence and you may become lost like Lehi said when he spoke of the mists of darkness.

> And I saw numberless concourses of people, many of whom were pressing forward, that they might obtain the path which led unto the tree by which I stood. And it came to pass that they did come forth, and commence in the path which led to the tree. And it came to pass that there arose a mist of darkness; yea, even an exceedingly great mist of darkness, insomuch that they who had commenced in the path did lose their way, that they wandered off and were lost (1 Nephi 8:21-23).

Then Nephi told us what the mist meant.

> And the mists of darkness are the temptations of the devil, which blindeth the eyes, and hardeneth the hearts of the children of men, and leadeth them away into broad roads, that they perish and are lost (1 Nephi 12:17).

You have commenced in the path that leads to the tree of life by being baptized and confirmed. Now you must take the Spirit for your guide and not become lost because of the temptations of the devil.

Another potential casualty of breaking the law of chastity is the loss of trust and respect of your future spouse. It is a wonderful experience to be able to tell your future spouse that you have kept yourself morally clean throughout your life. If, on the other hand, you need to tell him or her that you have not kept yourself morally clean, that may cause some difficulty. They may wonder if they can trust you, and their respect for you might waver. Why take that chance? Just keep yourself clean and you won't have to worry about it. There can also be friction that arises when one has been intimate with someone else and cannot help but compare the experiences. Even if this comparison is kept totally to oneself, their spouse may wonder about being compared. I have seen this factor alone cause great heartbreak and ultimately end in divorce.

What about your future children? If you did not keep the law of chastity while you were dating, are you going to feel uncomfortable if your son or daughter asks you about it? I have had two of my children ask me point-blank if I have always kept the law of chastity. Joyfully I could answer with a simple yes, but if I had had to tell them no, they might think therefore that it would be OK if they broke it. After all, Dad or Mom broke it, so what's the big deal? Avoiding that conversation it reason enough to closely keep the law of chastity.

Another problem with breaking the law of chastity is the potential delay in having a temple sealing for you and your spouse. It may take years before you can enter the temple and be sealed for eternity. You may have to go for a period of time without the blessing of taking the sacrament and renewing your covenants with the Lord.

Yet another serious result of breaking the law of chastity is the damage you can do to the person you are with. My brother had a roommate in college whose moral standard wasn't set very high. As a matter of fact, he had had several sexual partners and was frequently on the lookout for the next "conquest," as he used to call them. He set his sights on a beautiful daughter of God who had very high morals. It took him quite some time, but over several months he began to wear her down. Finally, he was successful in seducing her into a sexual act. His mission was accomplished and her standard was broken. Not too long after their encounter, they broke up and went their separate ways. The young girl felt so compromised that she felt she could not return to what she had been. She began to go out with other young men who wanted her for sex and she began to enjoy this new lifestyle. After some time, my brother's roommate had a change of heart and decided to go through the very difficult process of repentance. He humbled himself and talked to his priesthood authorities and began to seek the things of the Spirit. He felt so badly about what he had done to this particular girl that he sought her out and asked for her forgiveness. He explained to her that what he had done was very wrong and that she needed to repent and return to the wonderful wholesome girl she had been before he had beguiled her. Her response will probably haunt him for a long long time. She told him to forget it. She said that she liked her new lifestyle. She had no desire to change!

How do you think this young man felt? If he hadn't spent so much time breaking this young girl down, she may have remained clean until she met her husband-to-be and was sealed in the temple. Now it seems there is very little hope for that. This young man feels responsible! Can you carry a burden like that throughout your life? Do you want to have to stand before the Lord at the judgment day and report on what you did to negatively change the direction of the eternal life of one of His children? This kind of personal guilt is a heavy load to carry and is almost always associated with breaking the law of chastity.

Some other consequences of breaking the law of chastity could be any of a variety of venereal diseases or even AIDS. These diseases can not only cause dire illness, they can cause death! Of course you realize that when you have intercourse with someone, you are in a sense having intercourse with everyone that person has had intercourse with. Your partner might not have an illness, but they could be carrying one from someone else.

Many years ago, a man who was serving as one of my counselors in an elders quorum presidency told me about a man he knew who was basically a good member of the Church. This man went to a convention (his first) in a far-away city and was caught up in the glamour and thrill of the moment. He found himself drinking mixed drinks and getting a little tipsy. A young woman offered to help him get up to his hotel room. She took him to the room and convinced him to let her come in. Once in the room, she began to seduce him. He let his guard down and had sexual relations with her. In the morning, he awoke to an empty wallet and a note written in lipstick on the mirror of the bathroom which simply said—"WELCOME TO THE WORLD OF AIDS!" He may have given up his life for a simple moment of pleasure. He could lose his wife and children and end up suffering a slow, painful, lonely death simply because he wanted to have a few minutes of selfish indulgence! What a tragedy!

I think that you should look for a future spouse that has kept themselves just as clean as you have. That means that if you want someone who has remained virtuous throughout their life, you had better have the same to offer. It is not fair to think that one should be allowed to sew their wild oats and the other should fight the battles to keep themselves clean. Elder Bruce R. McKonkie once told me that if you have kept yourself morally clean all of your life, you should not settle for anything less in your spouse.

Now the last consequence of breaking the law of chastity that we will mention here is well put in the words of Alma to his son, Corianton.

> Now my son, I would that ye should repent and forsake your sins, and go no more after the lusts of your eyes, but cross yourself in all these things; for except ye do this ye can in nowise inherit the kingdom of God. Oh, remember, and take it upon you, and cross yourself in these things (Alma 39:9).

He tells us to cross ourselves, which cross-references to "Self Mastery" in the Topical Guide. If we don't do this, we cannot inherit the kingdom of God!!

Now for the assignment. CROSS YOURSELVES as pertaining to the lusts of the world and carefully consider the consequences of breaking the law of chastity. I list them here again just so you can look at them from time to time and remind yourself just how much is really at stake.

Consequences of breaking the law of chastity:

Pregnancy
Adoption
Premature Marriage
Maybe no chance for a mission
Loss of the Spirit

Loss of the trust of others
Loss of respect of others
Potential loss of a spouse that is morally clean
Possible delay of temple blessings
Possible restriction of taking the sacrament
Guilt for your sin
Guilt for altering the life of another child of God
Potential disease and illness
Possible physical death
Loss of potential to enter the kingdom of God

Gain your self-mastery in respect to your physical desires and resolve to never go over the line. Any one of the things in the list above or all of them could be your lot if you don't. MAKE THE RESOLVE RIGHT NOW BEFORE YOU CLOSE THE BOOK ON THIS CHAPTER THAT YOU WILL NOT STEP OVER THE LINE IN CONNECTION WITH THE LAW OF CHASTITY!

If you have already stepped over the line, read the next chapter.

6

Blessings Abound

There is a specific reason that the first sentence of Chapter 5 was to be sure to read Chapter 6. I want to make certain that you don't leave this book with the feeling that if you have broken the law of chastity that there is no hope! There is hope and there is the potential for exaltation in the eternities. Of course it is not without price and pursuit but it is well worth it!

Your Heavenly Father loves you more than you even love yourself or are loved by anyone on the earth. It is hard for me to imagine that there is a being that could love my children more than I do, but it is true. He loves you so deeply that he has prepared the way for you to repent of past transgressions and sins and move forward. The Atonement of Jesus Christ was brought about for all of us on the grounds of repentance. If you are willing to pay that price to give the burden of that sin to the Lord, you can be completely forgiven.

Do I really have to go to see the bishop?

In the book *The Miracle of Forgiveness*, President Spencer W. Kimball stated:

Many offenders in their shame and pride have satisfied their consciences, temporarily at least, with a few silent

prayers to the Lord and rationalized that this was suffi-
cient confession of their sins. 'But I have confessed my sin
to my Heavenly Father,' they will insist, 'and that is all
that is necessary.' This is not true where a major sin is
involved. Then two sets of forgiveness are required to
bring peace to the transgressor—one from the proper
authorities of the Lord's Church, and one from the Lord
himself. This is brought out in the Lord's clarification of
Church administration as he gave it to Alma:

'Therefore I say unto you, Go; and whosoever transgres-
seth against me, him shall ye judge according to the sins
which he has committed; and if he confess his sins before
thee and me, and repenteth in the sincerity of his heart,
him shall ye forgive, and I will forgive him also' (Mosiah
26:29) (Salt Lake City: Bookcraft, 1969, p. 179).

It is impossible for us to obtain forgiveness for major sin
without confessing to the proper church authority. We cannot
"will" it to be done. Our personal prayers, no matter how sin-
cere and how mighty they may seem, cannot totally free us
from serious sin. Contemplating a visit with the bishop for
breaking the law of chastity is extremely frightening, but it
should not be. If you think that you are going to be the first
and only person who confesses to your bishop about a serious
sin, think again. He may not have heard your story but it is
likely that during his service as the bishop he will have heard
several that are just as troublesome. You must know that he
wants to help you through the situation. His goal is your
peace of mind and spirit. He loves you and as your common
judge in Israel, he has the responsibility to assist you through
this difficult time.

You will probably have several thoughts run through your mind about how to bring it up to him. Of course, you will feel awkward and uneasy at first. But as soon as you have told him why you are there in his office, you will begin to feel the relief of that heavy burden being gently lifted from your shoulders! It doesn't really matter how you bring it up. You might say, "Bishop, I have committed a moral transgression and I need help," or, "Bishop, I have broken the law of chastity and I want to repent." Or anything else that is direct in letting him know what is going on and what you want to do about it. Most likely, you will immediately feel his love and understanding. He will ask you appropriate questions and guide you through the process of repentance. It may take a considerable amount of time but it is the only way to be restored to the peace of spirit that you previously had.

The bishop will also take your hand and guide you through the process of receiving forgiveness from the Lord You must receive forgiveness from both sources in order to be made whole again.

Taking that first step and talking to the bishop takes a lot of courage but you can do it. Remember that Satan will try to convince you not to go to the bishop! He knows that if he can keep you away from the bishop, he will likely be successful in keeping you away from Church activities and ultimately away from the Church itself. He will try to make you feel so guilty that you will lose all self-esteem. He would try to make you feel that you are no longer worthy to be considered one of God's children and that there is no way back to His presence. DON'T LET HIM WIN!

Now, if you have committed a sin and you're not sure if you need to talk to the bishop about it, GO AND TALK TO HIM! The bishop will tell you if it is something that requires his help. If it is, the process has begun. If it is not, he will guide you on how to proceed to find forgiveness from the Lord.

Finally, after you have received forgiveness from the Lord and the proper authorities of the Church, you must be willing to forgive yourself. Don't dwell on past sins! Drop them and move forward. If you have a problem with this, simply remind yourself that your priesthood leader, who is highly in tune with the Spirit, has seen to forgive you and the Lord Himself has forgiven you—are you more in tune than they? Probably not, so accept their forgiveness as reason enough to forgive yourself!

One final note here—if your sin does require confession to the bishop, you must make sure that you tell him everything that is causing you feelings of guilt. Lay it all out on the table. Don't try to hide anything because it will only come back to haunt you in the future. Don't leave his office thinking—I wonder if I should have told him about this or that? TELL HIM! He will tell you if you don't need to tell him anything further. When you seek the Lord's forgiveness, follow the same rule and tell Him everything! If you do this and the bishop forgives you on behalf of the Church and the Lord forgives you, you will feel totally clean. There will be no cobwebs in your heart.

Your bishop will normally have at least an annual visit with you at which time he will ask you some questions about your worthiness. It is easy to consider lying to avoid being embarrassed about something. Sometimes these interviews come quickly and you haven't had the time to prepare for a confession so you think, "I'll just lie this time and then I really will make an appointment and go and see him about it." President Kimball said this about lying to priesthood leaders.

> Those who lie to Church leaders forget or ignore an important rule and truth the Lord has set down: that when he has called men to high places in his kingdom and has placed on them the mantle of authority, a lie to them is tantamount to a lie to the Lord; a half-truth to his officials is like a half-truth to the Lord; a rebellion against his servants is comparable with a rebellion against the Lord; and any infraction against the Brethren who hold the gospel keys is a thought or an act against the Lord. As he expressed it: 'For he that receiveth my servants receiveth me; and he that receiveth me receiveth my father' (D&C 84:36-37) (*Miracle of Forgiveness*, p. 183).

Look at this interview as an opportunity to unload now and get the ball rolling. WHEN IS THE BEST TIME TO SET UP AN APPOINTMENT TO SEE THE BISHOP IF YOU HAVE BROKEN THE LAW OF CHASTITY? RIGHT NOW! If you have been involved in any transgression that you feel the bishop might need to be aware of, CALL HIM RIGHT NOW. I mean it! Put the book down and call him right now! Don't wait another moment—do it now!

The two main reasons that people delay talking to their bishop about transgressions are pride and embarrassment. Don't let pride or embarrassment keep you out of the celestial kingdom! Pride must be broken and embarrassment must be overcome. President Kimball said, "The transgressor must have a 'broken heart and a contrite spirit' and be willing to humble himself and do all that is required (*Miracle of Forgiveness* p. 179).

The process of repentance is not an easy road. It is not a principle which suggests that you can go and do what you want to and then spend a little time going through repentance and get it all taken care of. I do not know of a single person who has said that it was worth it to sin because the process of repentance wasn't a big deal. Almost without fail I have heard people say, "I wish I had never done what I did because the process of repentance was very difficult." Note that it is not impossible, but very difficult and very worth it! "Confession brings peace. How often have people departed from my office relieved and lighter of heart than for a long time! Their burdens were lighter, having been shared. They were free. The truth had made them free" (*The Miracle of Forgiveness* p. 187).

Now let's explore the great blessings of keeping the law of chastity.

Pregnancy—at the right time and in the right circumstances, this is one of the most sublime experiences of life for both a mother and a father. There are very few things in this life that compare with holding a new baby and feeling their soft skin and hearing their little squeaks. The satisfaction of knowing that they are born in the covenant and have the assurance of the blessings of Abraham is exhilarating.

Marriage—at the right time to a person who has kept themselves as you have kept yourself is the highest form of imitation of Godhood that we are allowed.

Mission—the ability to enter the mission field free of guilt and ready to work hard and be obedient will change almost every aspect of your life. What a blessing to be able to spread the gospel to your brothers and sisters throughout the world!

Companionship of the Spirit—receiving the guidance and help of the Spirit is a great blessing. Being worthy to receive promptings and then having the courage to follow them can teach us many things about being in the presence of God.

Having the trust of others gives you confidence and makes you feel like you can do anything in righteousness. You can become a person that people rely on to do the right thing.

Having the respect of others fills you with the desire to continue to do your best in every aspect of your life. You want to excel in school, church, and personal goals. You have an almost unquenchable positive attitude that will take you a long way in this life.

The opportunity of receiving temple blessings is literally of eternal significance. There are so many lessons to be learned in the temple by the Spirit that you can feel it change your life. It is very common to hear people say that they learn something new almost every time they go to the temple.

The blessing of taking the sacrament each Sunday and renewing your covenants with the Lord is a purifying and cleansing experience. If you bring your minor sins to sacrament and are truly repentant, you can leave sacrament meeting as clean as you left the waters of baptism!

Not having to carry the burden of guilt for your sin will make you feel light and fresh. The heavy burden of sin will not be upon you and you will feel as though you can do anything.

Not having to bear the guilt of altering the life of another child of God is a blessing as well. Those who carry those burdens think about them virtually every day and it can ruin their lives. It is a blessing not to have to deal with that.

Knowing you are free of illness or disease associated with the sins of morality is very reassuring. Several years ago, I had an unusual sore by my right eye. I went to the eye doctor to whom I was referred and, after examining it, he said that I should go and get tested for HIV (the AIDS virus). I was shocked! I went back to my family doctor who knows me quite well and asked him about the test. He laughed and said that he knew my wife and I well enough to know that there was no possibility of me having that disease unless I had had some kind of blood contact with someone who had it. I assured him that I had not and he told me not to bother with the test. If I had been breaking the law of chastity, I would have been tremendously concerned and would have taken the test, but knowing that that was not the case gave me the reassurance that I did not need to worry about having that disease.

Of course the greatest blessing of keeping the law of chastity is the potential to enter the kingdom of God. There is no greater blessing in Heaven or on Earth than being able to return to the presence of God and receive all of His blessings!

Now for your assignment. If you have had a problem with any moral transgression of any kind, GO AND SEE YOUR BISHOP! It's that simple. Start the process of passing that heavy burden onto the Lord and using His atoning sacrifice in your behalf.

7

Have Some Fun!

Here is a list of dating ideas that should keep you from ever saying, "I don't know what to do." Try some of these ideas and have some fun!

AQUARIUM
AMUSEMENT PARK
ARCADE
AIR SHOW
ART GALLERY
BADMINTON
BAKE COOKIES TOGETHER
BALLET
BARBECUES
BASEBALL GAME
BASKETBALL GAME
BATTING CAGES
BEACH
BEACH VOLLEYBALL
BIKE RIDING
BILLIARDS/POOL
BINGO
BIRD WATCHING
BLOOD DONATION
BOARD GAMES

BOATING

BOOKSTORES

BOWLING

BROOM BALL

BUILD A SNOWMAN

BUILD MODELS

CAMPING

CANOEING

CAR SHOW

CARD GAMES

CARVE A JACK-O-LANTERN

CAVES

CIRCUS

CITY PARK

CONCERT—(Appropriate music of course!)

COOK OUT

COUNTRY DRIVE

CRAFTS

DANCE LESSONS

DANCING

DECORATE A CHRISTMAS TREE

DEEP SEA FISHING

DINNER

DINNER THEATERS

FEED DUCKS AT A POND

FERRY BOAT RIDE

FINGER PAINT

FISHING

FLEA MARKETS

FLY A KITE

FOOTBALL GAME

FRISBEE

FRUIT PICKING
GO-CARTS
GOLF/FRISBEE GOLF
HAY RIDE
HELICOPTER RIDE
HIGH SCHOOL MUSICAL
HIKING
HIDE AND SEEK
HISTORIC SITE
HOBBY SHOW
HOCKEY GAME
HOPSCOTCH
HORSEBACK RIDING
HORSE RACES
HOT AIR BALLOON RIDE
ICE CREAM
ICE SKATING
ICE SKATING SHOW
INTERNET CAFÉ
JAZZ CONCERT
JET SKI
KARAOKE
KAYAKING
KICK THE CAN
LAKE
LAZAR TAG
MAKE DINNER TOGETHER
MAKE ICE CREAM
MAKE ICE CREAM SUNDAES
MAKE SNOW ANGELS
MIDNIGHT MOVIE
MINIATURE GOLF

MOON-LIT WALK
MOPED RIDING
MOVIE
MUSEUM
MUSICAL
NATURE WALK
OPERA
PAINT BALL
PLAY
POETRY READING
POPCORN
RACQUETBALL
RIVER TUBING
RIVERBOAT CRUISE
ROAST MARSHMALLOWS
ROCK CLIMBING
ROLLER BLADING/ROLLER SKATING
SAILING
SCAVENGER HUNT
SCUBA DIVING
SEA SHELL SEARCH ON THE BEACH
SKIING
SLEDDING
SNORKELING
SNOW BOARDING
SNOWMOBILING
SPORTING EVENT
STARGAZING
STEAM BOAT RIDE
STUDENT ART SHOWS AND PRODUCTIONS
STUDENT FAIRS
SURFING

SWIMMING
SYMPHONY
TAG
TENNIS
THUMB WRESTLE
TOBOGGANING
TOUCH FOOTBALL
TOURIST ATTRACTIONS
TRAMPOLINE
TREE CLIMBING
TUBING DOWN A RIVER
VIDEOS
VOLLEYBALL
VOLUNTEER AT A SOUP KITCHEN
WALKS
WATCH PLANES TAKE OFF AND LAND
WATCH THE SUNRISE
WATCH THE SUNSET
WATER-SKIING
WATER SLIDE
WHITE WATER RAFTING
WINDOW SHOPPING
WORKOUT TOGETHER
ZOO

Now for your assignment. HAVE FUN AND ENJOY DATING! IT CAN BE THE TIME OF YOUR LIFE!

Ice Breakers Game

Have you ever been on a blind date and wondered what to talk about? Did you ever wonder about what was going through your date's mind? Try ICE BREAKERS to break the ice!

Ice Breakers is a brief, very straight forward, fun game that will help you and your date get to know each other.

Simply draw a card and answer the question on the card. If you want to turn the question to your date for an answer, that's great, but be sure to answer it first yourself!

Just take a little time to break the ice and have a blast.

Cut along the dotted lines on the following pages to cut out each "Ice Breakers" card. Then draw a card and let the fun begin!

What is your
favorite food?

How much of it can
you eat in
one sitting?

If you could trade
places with anyone or
anything, who or
what would it be and
why?

If you could go for a
one-way ride in a time
machine, which time
period would you travel
to and why?
(Remember, it is only one-
way—you cannot return.)

What is your
favorite
thing to do?

What is your
favorite
scripture?

Tell a ghost
story.

Tell a funny story
about a friend.

What was your
most embarassing
moment?

Ice Breakers   Ice Breakers

Ice Breakers   Ice Breakers

Ice Breakers   Ice Breakers

Ice Breakers   Ice Breakers

If you were a food, what would you be and why?

If you were a pretzel, would you be straight or twisted and why?

If you could have left something in the time capsule that the astronauts left on the moon, what would it have been and why?

If you were one piece of a place setting, what would you be and why?

What is your favorite scripture story and why?

Who is your favorite person in the scriptures and why?

Who is your favorite superhero and why?

If you were a vegetable, what would you be and why?

Ice Breakers   Ice Breakers

Ice Breakers   Ice Breakers

Ice Breakers   Ice Breakers

Ice Breakers   Ice Breakers

Seen any good movies lately?

What is your favorite color?

Name an activity that you enjoy that you could still do with one hand and one foot tied behind your back.

If you were told that you had three days to live, what would you try to accomplish?

If you wrote a book, what would the title be?

If you were an animal, what would you be and why?

If you were a car, what kind would you be and why?

Who is your idol and why?

Ice Breakers   Ice Breakers

Ice Breakers   Ice Breakers

Ice Breakers   Ice Breakers

Ice Breakers   Ice Breakers

How many teams or clubs do you belong to and what do they do?

What is your favorite kind of dessert?

What was the hardest class you ever had and why?

What are the names & ages of all of the people in your family?

What do your parents do for a living?

What color is your hair, really?

What is the funniest thing that ever happened to you?

What is your favorite movie of all time?

Ice Breakers   Ice Breakers

Ice Breakers   Ice Breakers

Ice Breakers   Ice Breakers

Ice Breakers   Ice Breakers

Did you make your bed this morning?

Have you been to Disneyland? If so, what was your favorite ride?

From how many different countries have you met people?

What was the best gift you ever gave for Christmas and why?

What was the best gift you ever received for Christmas and why?

What is your favorite song?

What is your favorite musical group?

What is your favorite sport?

Ice Breakers   Ice Breakers

Ice Breakers   Ice Breakers

Ice Breakers   Ice Breakers

Ice Breakers   Ice Breakers

About the Author

Lyman Hinckley Rose was born in Salt Lake City, Utah, on September 4, 1958, to Ford Thomas Rose and Beulah Hinckley Rose. He served a mission in the Australia Sydney Spanish Mission.

He graduated from Brigham Young University in April 1985 with a degree in business finance, and he owns his own business.

He has taught Missionary Preparation for nine years on both the stake and college institute level, and developed his own curriculum in an attempt to satisfy the needs of the students in the class.

He married the former Lesa Peterson on March 15, 1982. They have nine children and reside in Bountiful, Utah.

He has served in many positions in the Church, but his passion has always been missionary work. As a family the Roses enjoy family and outdoor activities.